Squat Wisely

Reflections for the Body and Mind

Kristen A. Hester

Contents

Acknowledgments

Look, Ma! I did it! If you are reading this, it means that your words have come to pass. Your Ashley is a published author now! Thank you for continuously seeing my potential when I did not. Thank you for being my constant cheerleader throughout every endeavor of my life. Thank you for encouraging me and building me up. I love you.

Daddy, from youth to adulthood, I thank you for consistently being a father that I can count on. I'm thankful that you never fail to see the best in me. I'm thankful that you always believe in my mind and my abilities. I'm thankful that you always support my business endeavors through both your encouragement and your presence. I love you.

Thank you both for coming in and lifting my burdens away. You invited me back to where my life began. You revived my soul. You helped to heal my tired mind. The tears fall as I type this because before life could break me, you both stepped in and strengthened me.

So, thank you both for your discernment. Thank you both for every prayer you have spoken over my life. Thank you both for reminding me that I don't have to fight in this life alone. Thank you both for being love in action. Thank you both for your wisdom. It has helped to shape my mind and the person and woman I have become.

In so many ways, I am a reflection of you. As you are proud of me, I am abundantly proud of you. I always tell my students that my parents are the wisest people I know. That will never change, and neither will my love for you.

Introduction

"You're going to write a book one day." These are the words my mother declared long ago. Before I believed it, she spoke it and planted a seed within me. That seed has manifested into the very words you are reading right now. I always enjoyed writing when I was younger, but as an adult, the idea of writing a book felt more daunting. It is 2024 now, and I actually began the plan to write a book in 2015. I even hired a book editor. I would begin but never felt solid about what I was typing.

As someone who has a deep passion for the art of speaking, I feel that anytime I am asked to speak, I have an obligation to share something of substance--something that can heal and uplift. When I am preparing to speak, I don't begin by writing.

Once the urgency hits me, I proceed to record myself, beginning by speaking from my soul. If what I have recorded does not move me to tears, or at least teaches me something that impresses myself, then it's not moving me. Therefore, I know it won't move others. I won't share anything I create until I am deeply moved by it and it resonates with my heart and my soul.

This aspect transferred over to my writing. I did not want to write a book just to say I wrote one. Like my speaking, I want this book to speak to your soul, speak to *our* soul. Even if only one chapter from this book resonates deeply for you, I would be thankful for that alone.

So, feel free to take your time with this book. Each chapter is a reflection for either the body or the mind, and some chapters reflect both the body and mind. You can read this book in any order. If one chapter title calls your name, spend a week or longer just focused on that one chapter if you like. Each chapter will have a Squat Challenge at the end and a Wise Act to reflect on and execute.

For the Squat Challenges, always maintain proper form. You can search YouTube for a visual example of each squat by entering the name of the squat from the Squat Challenge. If you're already familiar with the squat variation, feel free to perform it safely when time allows.

Afterward, always engage in some gentle full-body stretches. You can find videos to guide you by searching "Gentle Full Body Stretch" on YouTube.

The Squat Challenges and Wise Acts are not mandatory to enjoy the book; they're simply another way to gain a new perspective or experience. I've encountered daily action steps in books before and didn't always complete them as I read. Instead, I took mental notes and later incorporated the ones that resonated with me. You can do the same.

This is a stress-free book, and I allow it to be whatever it needs to be for your life. All I know is this: My book was released at this exact time to reach you during this particular moment in your life. In fairness, what resonates for me may not resonate for others, and I acknowledge that. I simply thank you for considering my book, and I hope that after completing it, you will at least be reminded to always *Squat Wisely*.

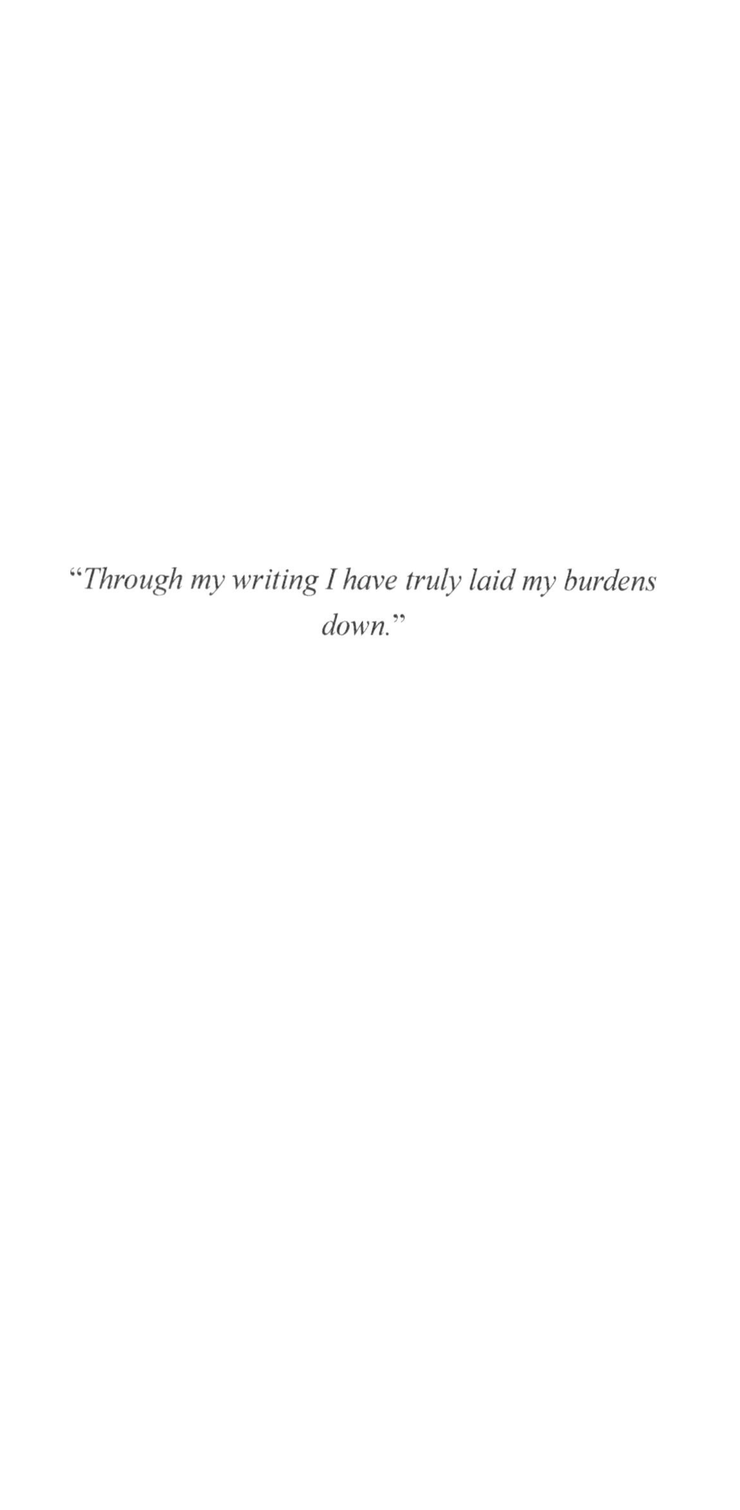

"Through my writing I have truly laid my burdens down."

Chapter 1
Write It Out

I remember when I was a kid, and my mom bought me a diary that had a lock and key. It made me feel so grown up to have my own private book of thoughts. Fast forward many years later to me being a full-grown adult, I decided to revisit my youth and get a diary. This time, a more adult version. One where you have to put in a numerical code to unlock it.

You know how people say just the act of going to the doctor magically seems to cure what had been bothering you for weeks. You put it off, saying it will get better. Yet, it seems like it won't shake, so you finally break down and go to the doctor. Once you're in for your evaluation, all of a sudden, the aches and pains have subsided. Or, that stubborn cold has finally resolved itself.

I liken this to writing. More specifically, therapeutic writing. The next time you are at your angriest or most frustrated self, I want you to put all of your thoughts to paper. It is imperative that you keep it old-school by putting pen to paper. I know we all have cool devices these days, but old-fashioned writing makes this writing experience more effective.

Now, I want you to write everything. I mean EVERY-thing. Do not censor yourself. I don't care how dark, how depressing, how vulgar, how sick, write it all down. You can write as harshly as you need to. You want this writing session to be as honest and authentic as possible. To the point that if someone were to see it, it would make you and the reader cringe.

That won't happen, so do not hold back. If fears are consuming you, write about that. If intrusive thoughts are crippling you, write about it. If you're angry at your-self, write about that. If you're angry with a spouse, a friend, a child, a parent, your pet even, write about it. If you're upset about your job or your business, put words to those feelings.

Write every frustration. Write every annoyance. Write every hurt. Write every disappointment. If the tears fall, let them soak onto the paper. You're doing soul work. There is a saying that talks about laying down your burdens. As you write unapologetically, you're not only laying your burdens down, you are lifting yourself up to a place of healing on the other side of your brutal honesty.

Because after you've written it all out, I want you to rip up the paper and throw it away. This is symbolic to release those burdens from your life. Its purpose has been fulfilled. You see it differently now compared to before. You can do this in your parked car at the park. Or, anywhere that you feel safe in that moment with a trash can nearby to dispose of your ripped-up writing.

I should note that there are journals and writings that I feel we should keep. I still have some of my old journals, and I reflect back on those writings, and I see where I may have grown or even where I may have remained the same. However, the writing I am referring to in this chapter is more like therapeutic shadow work writing. This is when you allow yourself to boldly confront yourself so you can uplift yourself to a place of healing and empowerment.

Writing in this way is profound because there have been numerous times where I have really gone there by writing it all out. I mean the hard stuff. The stuff we don't dare address with others nor ourselves. And a lot like going to the doctor, and feeling well all of a sudden, the act of simply writing it all out leads to a sudden shift. The situation may still be the same. But how I see the situation or, most importantly, how I experience the situation has changed in some profound way. All of a sudden what felt heavy is now light.

Through my writing I have truly laid my burdens down. So, I encourage you to do the same thing. This is vital for your mental fitness. So much from childhood, like writing in a diary, is essential for our overall well-being. As a kid, I made time to write, play, and even imagine myself in cool and different ways. We have to go back to the innocence of our youth, kind of a journeying back to the root of ourselves because in those simple things we enjoyed as kids, we can find our strength and our healing there.

So, write it out. I mean this literally. All of that anger, resentment, disappointment, write it OUT of you. Aggressively take all those hard truths from pen to paper. Write it out, then throw it out and EXPECT the shift that I know WILL follow.

Squat Challenge

Option 1:

30 Bodyweight Squats Straight Through

Option 2:

3 Sets of 10 Bodyweight Squats
Rest In-Between Sets for 15-seconds

Wise Act

Go buy yourself a brand new spiral notebook. Intentionally put it in a special place so you will always know where it is. Reserve using it until you NEED to Write it OUT. Let that Notebook serve as a reminder for both acknowledging and letting go of your burdens.

6

"I have grown to realize that it doesn't matter if somebody out there isn't pleased; the bigger questions are: Am I pleased? Am I okay with how I'm living?"

Chapter 2
The Watcher

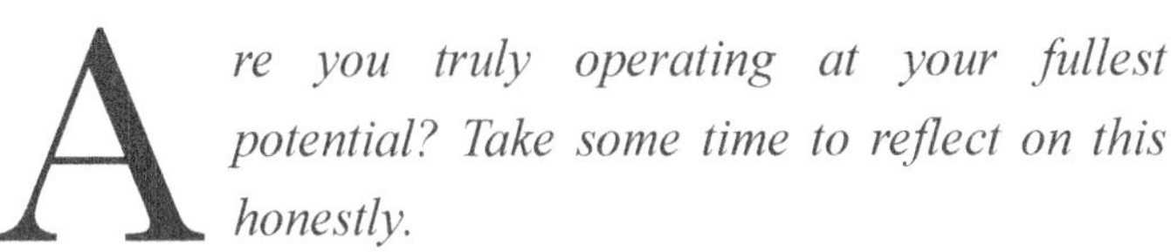

Are you truly operating at your fullest potential? Take some time to reflect on this honestly.

During the start of my fitness career, I learned a profound lesson about myself and my ability to truly operate at my fullest potential. Some days, I strive towards that, and I'm successful, and some days I'm not. Whitney Houston has a song that says, "I didn't know my own strength." That line alone speaks to so many areas of not only my fitness life but my life in general.

I recognized my own strength and lack thereof while preparing for my fitness classes at home. I'd often lose focus after just 10 minutes of practice. I'd either feel tired, distract myself by getting something to drink, or end up on Facebook. Eventually, I'd resume exercising.

However, after 5 or 10 minutes, exhaustion would set in again.

I found it fascinating how different my experience was when I attended class. Despite struggling to practice for even 10 minutes at home, once I arrived at the gym, it felt like a whole other person had taken over. I was fully energized from start-to-finish. Of course, there were days when I felt sluggish, especially if I hadn't eaten breakfast or rested properly. On those occasions, my energy levels weren't as high as I would have liked. Yet, even during those moments, something inside me pushed through the entire hour. However, I'm that same person who's at home, and after 10 minutes, I'm ready to lay down. My focus at home is all over the place, and because it's all over the place, it weakens my potential.

Interestingly, there is something very profound about not having laziness as an option. I repeat, there is something *very* profound about not having laziness as an option. See, when you're at home, you're comfortable, right? When you don't have the so-called overseer, just yourself, you're too comfortable. But when you must deliver, laziness is not an option. It's like your body knows it's not an option; your mind knows it's not an option; your actions know it's not an option. You either do or you die; you either quit, or you're going to make it happen.

It's funny because fitness is like that. Of course, I'm the fitness instructor, so I better deliver, right? That's what they hired me for. But even in your own personal fitness journey, whatever it is you're trying to do in terms of building muscle or dropping weight, it's still the same game.

I hired a personal trainer when I first started my fitness journey. I hired one because I wasn't personally motivated to get up and do the work myself. I just wasn't going to do it. I've never been a fan of going to the gym to work out anyway. So, if I was going to work out and be productive, the trainer had to come to my house. I had to invest that money because once I put my money to it, then I knew I would do something about it.

Just as our money can propel us into action, having all eyes on us can do the same. When I must deliver, and laziness is not an option, there's that something that wakes up inside of you. That's your potential. That's your willpower.

Think about this: If you are someone like me who struggles to constantly keep the house clean 24/7, let people say that they are about to come over and spend the night. Oh my goodness, your house will look gorgeous, right? Where does all that motivation come from? How is it that you're Miss or Mister Clean all of a sudden? It's because you know people are going to be in your house, and you don't want them to think that you comfortably live any kind of way. So, you're very motivated to tidy up. You're very motivated to put on a good front. Now that people are showing up and looking, you easily realize...laziness is NOT an option.

This reminds me of a nugget of wisdom I gained from the book titled *The Power of Now* by Eckhart Tolle. The book discusses the importance of being a watcher of ourselves. Often, we act differently when we believe someone is observing us. For instance, if we expect guests to visit, suddenly we feel the need to ensure our house looks impeccable. Similarly, when I have to lead a full-hour workout session, I must awaken something within myself to deliver what I've been hired to do. Why? Because people are watching; someone is observing. This observation prompts effort and unlocks potential.

The Power of Now suggests you need to become that person. You need to become the watcher of yourself. You need to tidy up the house because it's your house; it's where you dwell. Don't make it stunning for outsiders; make it comfortable for the person who dwells there daily. Just delivering a great fitness class because participants will be showing up, eager and ready to go isn't enough. I had to reverse that mindset.

I'm representing myself; I'm watching! I have a certain standard for myself. So, when I go to class, I need to deliver not only for the participants, but for myself as well. But, how do I accomplish this? It starts with what I do at home first. I can't get comfortable and after 10 minutes of practice take a nap or check Facebook.

In order to self-correct distracting behaviors, we have to get to the place where we are more the watcher of ourselves, and we have to be uncomfortable with what we think of ourselves. We're more uncomfortable with what someone else thinks. We are more uncomfortable with what the job thinks. Or, the people visiting from out of town.

We are motivated to change because of some outside eyes. But the wise way to bring out the best potential inside of you is when you become the watcher of yourself. When you become the person who you want to please the most. When you become the person who you want to make the most proud. It's your life that you're living. You are your best judge and representative.

So, even if you have a fitness goal for yourself, ensure that it's a goal driven primarily by your own desires rather than external influences. During my preparation for the personal trainer exam, we studied the concepts of intrinsic and extrinsic goals. Consider clients aiming to shed weight solely to please a spouse; their success may be hindered not by lack of effort but by the source of their motivation.

Their drive often originates from seeking external validation rather than finding internal satisfaction; it's extrinsic rather than intrinsic. While it's natural to prioritize our well-being for the sake of loved ones, the key lies in genuinely embracing these health goals as our own. Without this personal connection, we risk reverting to old habits. This principle extends beyond health; whether in business, career, or any other endeavor, intrinsic motivation fuels lasting success.

As you embark on your fitness journey, you'll uncover your strengths. This sentiment echoes the wisdom found in Whitney Houston's lyrics, highlighting the discovery of our untapped strengths. Additionally, there's a video by Will Smith where he unfolds lessons learned from reading and running, which you can find on YouTube.

I prefer not to spoil the video for you. I encourage you to seek it out because I believe it's truly inspiring. It mirrors the sentiment expressed by Whitney Houston earlier in the chapter. When you push yourself, even if it's just a small achievement like walking an extra lap at your local park, celebrate it. Remember, those baby steps are actually significant strides, especially in fitness.

You're much stronger than you think you are. I remember the very first time I started working out with a personal trainer. The first time we met, I was so, so sick. Working in the fitness industry is the closest thing to working in the medical field, if you ask me. It's serious business. When you get into cardio and you're getting your heart rate up, that can be fatal if you're not careful. That's why people who lead group fitness and personal training sessions have to complete various certifications, including CPR.

Fitness can be intense. Participants in some of my classes have said to me: "I think I'm about to die!" You hear that a lot at the gym because, honestly, that's kind of what it feels like. Especially if you have low cardio endurance and you're not used to working out, you'll find yourself huffing and puffing, getting hot, and sweating. This can be very overwhelming and a shock to your body.

Although fitness can be intense, it's also life-changing because it does a lot of great things for your health. Just go at an easy pace and start in a safe zone so you don't put yourself in a dangerous situation. When I started working out, I think back on those early days, and I look at where I am now. I remember how sick I felt, how I DID feel like I was about to die. And I do some of the same things now that I was doing back then. I almost laugh at my older self from when I first started out because I'm amazed at the things that I couldn't handle back then. That just proves that your fullest potential is always within you.

I'm still that same person from years ago, just stronger, wiser, and more knowledgeable about fitness compared to when I first started this journey. The potential was always there; I simply had to tap into consistency to bring it out.

Now, what about you? Consider the goals you have for your life. Reflect on the desires you hold for your health, business, and even your home life. Contemplate how you can redirect your focus from external influences back to your own aspirations. Remember, your home is your dwelling place, and your body is your vessel. Be the watcher of yourself; don't let external perceptions guide you. When you notice yourself succumbing to external pressures -- and I'm talking to myself too -- prompt yourself and consider: Are you living your life for those eyes, or will you take your power back and remind yourself that you are the watcher of your own life?

I have grown to realize that it doesn't matter if somebody out there isn't pleased; the bigger questions are: Am I pleased? Am I okay with how I'm living? Am I okay with the things that I do to my body? Am I okay with the way I honor or dishonor my home? Is it about the people who are going to come and visit, or is it about the person who takes up residence there daily?

You must be the watcher of yourself; don't only become uncomfortable when outsiders are watching. Instead, learn self-discipline and self-correction. When that becomes the focus, you will naturally tap into the power of your fullest potential because you are fully the watcher of yourself.

Squat Challenge

Option 1:

30 Jump Squats Straight Through

Option 2:

3 Sets of 10 Jump Squats
Rest In-Between Sets for 15-seconds

To Modify: Perform a Squat to Calf Raise Exercise to
Eliminate the Jump

Wise Act

I want you to duplicate a project I had to complete for a
Sociology class I took in college. My paper was titled:
The Sociology of Me. I was asked to take notice of how I
behaved when out in society and to write about it. I had
fun writing that paper and recognizing how both myself
and others tend to avoid eye contact when in public,
especially on elevators. Unlike myself, you don't have to

write a paper. Instead, let this serve as your **Be the Watcher** training. Let it groom your mind to do good, not because others are watching, but because *you* are.

"Even in the face of difficulty, observe how you're still ***holding yourself up.****"*

Chapter 3
Plank Wisdom

One of the best exercises for physical and mental fitness is the traditional forearm plank. It is one of those exercises clients often tell me looks easy when watching someone else do it but is actually harder than it looks. Planks work on the core to help stabilize and elevate your overall body weight. Many people cheat during forearm planks when it gets hard by sticking their butt up too high, but the objective is to maintain a straight line with your body, without letting the butt fly up too high.

I have to psych myself out to do planks for a long period of time. This is where mental fitness kicks in. If I play a song that keeps me pumped, I can plank much longer than I can without music playing. The music takes my focus off the plank, but at the same time, it helps me engage in the plank position for a longer duration. When performing bodyweight exercises, we sometimes take for granted just how much we are able to support ourselves.

Planking is widely regarded as a challenging exercise for good reason. I would argue that it beautifully and profoundly mirrors the complexities of life. If you're new to planking or haven't done it in a while, I encourage you to prepare your mind to perform a plank safely and with proper form. If you're already familiar with planks, you're likely aware of the importance of proper form, especially for the forearm plank. If you're uncertain, you can find helpful videos on YouTube by searching for "Forearm Plank". Watching these videos will give you a visual demonstration. Just remember the key points mentioned earlier about not letting your butt fly up too high and maintaining a straight line with your body.

If the traditional Forearm Plank is too advanced, search for "Modified-Forearm Plank" or "Beginner-Plank" on YouTube and give that a try. Now, as you do your planks, follow these instructions:

1. For the first plank, try for 15 seconds.
2. If 15 seconds is your limit, do three planks at 15 seconds each.

3. If 15 seconds feels too easy, on the second plank, try for 30 seconds.
4. If 30 seconds is your limit, do three more planks at 30 seconds each.
5. If 30 seconds feels too easy, try three more planks at one minute each.

Of the three durations, 15 seconds, 30 seconds, or one minute, decide which one was the most challenging, and perform an additional plank for that duration. For example, if 15 seconds was truly the most challenging, do one more plank for 15 seconds.

Take note of a few things while that plank presents its challenge, demanding your full mental, physical, and sometimes emotional effort to push through. Yet, *even in the face of difficulty, observe how you're still holding yourself up.* Indeed, you might think to yourself, "I can't do this much longer." I have a client who proves herself wrong every time she performs a plank. She always says to me, "I can't do this!" But her body and mind are proving her words wrong. While a plank is just another effective exercise, it also serves as a reminder of how we face challenges in life. As long as we're alive, we'll encounter challenges, and in the midst of it, we might tell ourselves, "I cannot handle this. This is too much for me." Just as planks remind us that we're stronger than we think, the challenges in life are similar. If we can push through planks when they get hard, we can push through the problems in our lives when they become hard as well.

Just as I put my music on to prepare my mind for intense exercise, it would be wise for us to approach our problems with the same mindset. Prepare your mind for the obstacles ahead by having a song in mind that helps you not only push through planks but also through life when it gets rough. Cultivate an internal dialogue that repels any self-defeating thoughts before the problems hit, ensuring you have a prepared plan of action when life's difficulties attempt to shake and break you. Be the same force of support for yourself in the face of life challenges as you are when planking. We are always much stronger than we think; here and now, we have no idea what we could face down the road. So, purpose-fully take note of the times when life was hard, but you survived it. We often like to forget the hard days, but remembering our struggles gives us a reminder of our strength when even tougher times arise.

Squat Challenge

Option 1:

1-minute Squat Pulses

Option 2:

Two 30-second Sets of Squat Pulses
Rest In-Between Sets for 15-seconds

Wise Act

Find yourself a fight song. A song you go to that helps you to fight the hard times that life can bring. If you already have one, find another to add to your playlist. One of my favorite songs is called *Believer* by Imagine Dragons. Check it out. It might become one of your favorite fight songs too.

24

"It is a shame to travel the road of success and never be corrected along the way."

Chapter 4
Wake-Up Call

"You've let yourself go." These were the words my doctor told me many years ago, words that stung worse than a bee in that moment. Though I was initially upset and taken aback, it was the wake-up call that I needed.

I have taught Philosophy at the college level for many years, and I've always been intrigued by how deeply engaged we become when faced with challenges or disagreements. Teaching Philosophy on campus is a completely different experience from teaching online. While I value both methods, I particularly enjoy being in-person because it allows me to witness my students' passion up close. Philosophy encompasses many controversial topics, and with controversy comes both passionate and heated discussions.

If students were on the same page, engagement was less involved. However, as soon as someone challenged another's outlook, listening and engagement were quickly heightened. This is not limited to the classroom; the same is true in our engagement with others, especially when we receive negative feedback, whether at work, from a loved one, or a friend. Our ears tend to zero in on all the negative points as we overlook the fact that some good was sprinkled in with the negative.

When my doctor told me, "you've let yourself go," I was so fixated on how direct his words were in that moment that I missed the fact that in the same conversation he also suggested tools for me to regain control of my weight.

He was not a medical professional trying to push prescriptions and repeat visits on me. Instead, he gave me tools to empower myself to live a healthier and more accountable life. It has been said that "exercise is the medicine" that many of us need. Along with amping up our physical activity, we can tackle many potential health concerns by moving more and eating less.

I am thankful for my doctor because his words not only ignited my weight loss, but it eventually opened the door for me to become a Certified Group Fitness Instructor and Certified Personal Trainer. The next time you receive feedback and you know that it's not coming from a hurtful place, purpose to listen with an open mind and see the opportunity that feedback has presented you with.

I remember leaving that doctor's appointment with tears in my eyes. I had tears, not because of what was said or how it was said, but because I realized it was true. I had let myself go. Furthermore, long before that doctor's appointment, I had another doctor's appointment.

I first started teaching on campus and took a break from it to focus on a different career path outside of education. After some years of working my other career, I found myself back into teaching, but online this time. Online college teaching was booming, and there was a great need for me to do it full-time. So, I put in my two weeks' notice and left my other career to work from home. Around the time of my transition, I had my annual check-up with my OB-GYN doctor. I was so excited to tell her that I was leaving my full-time corporate job to work from home in my pajamas. She was happy for me, but with a warning. As an OB-GYN, she deals with many moms who leave corporate to become full-time moms.

She said one thing that many of them have in common is that they tend to gain weight when they make that transition. So, she warned me about packing on the pounds. Fast forward some time later, she was right. I was at the "let myself go" stage. The weight was not extreme, but still too much for my height, and heavier than what I was accustomed to. Even then, my OB-GYN was a forewarning of what was to come, but because it was not a reality at the time, I did not take heed until I was forced to. Sometimes, wake-up calls come when we are so far gone that we *must* listen, while at other times, they come before we get too far gone and *should* listen.

Welcome the wake-up calls that come, and take heed to genuine correction. A mentor once told me: *It is a shame to travel the road of success and never be corrected along the way*. I'll add that self-correction is just as profound, if not more profound, than correction from others. When we recognize that we can make better choices and decisions with our lives, we are living out self-accountability. When we can embrace sincere feedback and correction from others, we understand that growth can happen through both internal as well as external means.

There is a quote that says, "Listening is a skill and a gift. Give generously." In my experience, I've found this to be true. When my students have disagreed with each other, they've actually learned and listened the most during those moments. To challenge or refute someone, you must first attentively listen to their perspective.

Because without truly hearing, you can't effectively engage or challenge.

Now that I think about it, my students always said the best classes were the ones where things got heated. Sure, we all love purposeful drama at times, but more than that, when our emotions rise, we feel more alive. As crazy as it sounds, I am glad when something moves me to tears, or even when I am angered by something, because it reminds me that I am alive and still have work to do. It points me back to my passions, or those flaws within that I need to face and conquer. These wake-up calls, though painful at times, not only pierce us but also puncture and destroy the bubbles that shield and blind us from liberating truths.

So, don't decline or block your wake-up calls. Instead, respond by fully engaging those moments and asking yourself: What am I to learn from this and how can I use this to help me grow?

Squat Challenge

Option 1:

40 Sumo Squats

Option 2:

4 Sets of 10 Sumo Squats
Rest In-Between Sets for 15-seconds

Wise Act

Purpose to seek out feedback from someone you may be hesitant to approach. Often, feedback catches us off guard, especially if it's negative. The wise actively seek out feedback, placing themselves in the line of fire. Be brave and embrace any wake-up calls that may follow.

"You may not feel like it yet, but you're ready."

Chapter 5
Misunderstood

One of the greatest lessons life and living has taught me is to be okay with being misunderstood. It has taken me a long time to grow to this place. And if I am being honest, times still arise where I care what others think more than I should. However, the older I become, the less I allow it to consume my life. With age, I have come to realize that some people will always think they have you all figured out.

Years ago, I was a new addition to a singing group. Around that time, I was also trying to establish myself as a speaker. Our group was starting a fundraiser and they asked us to consider promoting our services if we had a business. So, I placed an ad for my speaking. When our fundraiser book was published, one of the ladies in the group saw a video of me speaking, and she went on and on about how she could not believe I was speaking that way.

Personally, I was surprised by her shock because she doesn't know me any more than I know her. She could be a surgeon or own a bakery for all I know, and I would not be surprised because I do not know her or what her life entails. That goes to show even when we are minding our business, people will draw unfounded conclusions about us. If I'm going to be fair, I am certain I have done the same, but reflecting on this urges me to ask of myself: Why have I done this? Most importantly, with no reasons to support my conclusions.

Now, this is fair to challenge in those cases where we sincerely do not know much about the person. Interestingly, there are people who can say with reason that they know us. Like our relatives and close friends. Yet, even they do not know us to the extent that they think they do. That is not necessarily a bad thing. It is just the reality of life.

We can take others out of the picture and add ourselves. I know for a fact that I have done things where I have surprised myself. For example, I had a big fear of driving as a teen. Who would have thought I would have become a Driving Instructor? I was the most unlikely person to even think about working out. I am surprised that I have taught Group Fitness classes and trained Personal Training clients for years. That was so very far from who I thought I was. I could go on and on, but of course, you get my drift here.

Like anything else, there are pros and cons to this. On one hand, we need to awaken new awareness within ourselves. It stretches us and helps us connect with new possibilities, learning things that never crossed our minds before. On the other hand, it's sometimes wise to remain the same depending on the circumstance. For example, how many of us have purchased one of our old-time favorites from the store, only to find it labeled as "new and improved"? Sometimes, it truly is improved, while other times it was better left unchanged. Some surprises are worthwhile, and some not so much.

Even during times when I've surprised myself or shocked people who assumed they knew me, I've appreciated the lessons that come from being misunderstood and discovering behaviors or abilities in myself that I never knew existed.

I was at work one day, and I have always been an old soul because most of my friends at work were always older people. I was talking to one of my older buddies, and we would have deep discussions about life, music, and anything else that would come up. Music is what sparked our work relationship. Amy Winehouse was a newer artist at the time, and everyone was talking about her. My work buddy is named Tony. Tony said, "She's trying to be like Dusty Springfield." From there, Tony would bring me Dusty Springfield records, and that sparked us talking about music, life, and more.

Tony was one of those guys who was misunderstood, and I know for a fact he was abundantly okay with that. He is a New Yorker with a strong accent and thick, long dark hair. He would have road rage with people in the parking deck. People would tell me, "Get your crazy friend!" But if you looked beyond what some people labeled as crazy and you took the time to actually speak to Tony, you would explore a lot of wisdom.

One day we got on the subject of death. I have no idea how we even got there, but it is some wisdom that I still think about and reflect on today. I remember telling him how I don't fear my own death. However, I do fear how I would handle the death of my mom or my dad. I remember Tony saying to me not to worry about that because if or when that happens, I will be ready when it does. I'm actually getting teary-eyed typing this right now, but he told me nothing like that can happen until you are ready for it to.

The misunderstood nature of life is not limited to people and their perceptions of us. We all know that life comes with its highs and its lows. Those difficult moments are some of the most misunderstood moments of our lives. But if we reflect on those events, we realize that we have survived them all up to this point. Sure, we may not have felt ready at the time, but the fact that we are still standing means that we were able to withstand it regardless of how we may have felt.

So, welcome the misunderstood moments that life can bring. Whether others are projecting their opinions onto you, whether you are underestimating your capabilities, or whether life presents you with painful moments such as death, sickness, or any struggle that you find difficult to comprehend, just remember, you have survived every misunderstanding and hardship up to this point. If you handled it then, you can handle it now. *You may not feel like it yet, but you're ready.*

Squat Challenge

Option 1:

1 Minute Squat to Alternating Knee Lift

Option 2:

2 Sets of 30-second Squats to Alternating Knee Lift
Rest In-Between Sets for 15-seconds

Wise Act

Consider reaching out to someone you've misjudged or underestimated. Regardless of their awareness of your feelings, communicate your respect for them via your preferred method—whether in person, through email, or text. Acknowledge any misjudgments you've made, sincerely apologize, and highlight the ways they've proven you wrong.

Why? Because undoubtedly, someone has misjudged you too. While we don't live for others' recognition, we all appreciate when people openly acknowledge and correct their mistakes. So, you be that example and brighten someone's day.

"People will always have something to say."

Chapter 6
Squat...Highly

Maybe the title of the book gave it away, but the traditional bodyweight squat is my favorite exercise. So, let's focus on squats and why I think they're effective.

Before I unfold my personal experience with squats, it's crucial to acknowledge that everyone's body responds differently to exercise. While my journey is unique to me, it may offer insights that could benefit your own fitness journey.

Now, let's rewind to 2014-2015 when I first embarked on my weight loss goals. For years, I've been working from home, leading a sedentary lifestyle that contributed to weight gain. Despite not having the craziest diet, the lack of activity made it easy for me to gain the extra pounds.

When I recognized the need for change, I decided to invest in an exercise bike and hire a personal trainer. Interestingly, many people encounter a similar situation where they do everything right but fail to see results or hit a sudden plateau. Despite diligently following all the right steps, the weight was not moving. While seeking solutions, I turned to YouTube and stumbled upon someone undergoing a similar journey. This individual had discovered a squat challenge that encouraged 100 squats a day for 30 days. So, I decided to give it a try.

At the time, I was not a fitness professional; I was just a girl trying to lose weight. Although my form was horrible, the cool thing about it was that I actually saw results. I did before and after photos. I focused especially on the back of my legs--the area where women get the dimply skin, or, to be more exact, cellulite. During that 30-day period, I had these shorts that I took my photos in, and I would wear those shorts periodically.

I always tell people not to rely solely on the scale to measure their progress because sometimes it goes up, and sometimes it goes down. Instead, focus on how you feel in your body and how your clothes fit. That alone indicates you're likely losing inches, even if the weight isn't dropping. You're gradually getting closer to your goal. So, that's what I noticed.

I wore those shorts and felt they fit much better, but I refrained from comparing before and after until after the 30-day period. When I compared those photos, I was surprised. More than anything else, doing those 100 squats a day became a game-changer for me. I saw results, more definition in my legs, and even that dimply area of skin was smoothing out.

Now, one reason why squats are effective is that they target very large muscle groups--your quadriceps, glutes, and hamstrings. By working and fatiguing these large muscles, you naturally start to burn more fat over-all, making squats a wise choice for many. So, if you feel like you've hit a plateau and aren't getting the most out of your workouts, consider incorporating more squats into your routine, or start including them if you're not already doing so.

If you're feeling too busy to work out, squats offer a no-excuse solution. They're versatile and easily integrated into your daily routine. For instance, try incorporating 10 squats each time you visit the restroom. If you have a spare minute, set a timer on your phone and dedicate it to squats. Whether you're in a restroom stall or working from home, squats provide a convenient way to stay active.

Furthermore, squats are suitable for most fitness levels. However, it's crucial to emphasize the importance of maintaining proper form while performing squats. You can search for videos on proper squat form on YouTube to ensure you're executing the exercise correctly. Listening to your body is also essential to avoid overuse injuries, especially if attempting the 100 squats a day challenge.

There's no shame in doing it only 1, 2, or 3 days a week to keep your joints healthy. You always want to ensure that you're cautious about protecting your knees during squats. One common cue is to envision yourself sitting back into a chair, a technique particularly useful for beginners and seniors new to exercise.

The goal is to shift the weight of your body behind you, avoiding excessive pressure on your joints by not pushing your body weight forward. Instead, aim to distribute your weight onto the heels of your feet. To achieve this, push your hips back, moving your buttocks backward, while keeping your chest up to prevent hunching forward. As you lower yourself into the squat position, ensure you can see your toes. Always be mindful not to let your knees extend beyond your toes during the squat movement.

Again, when I began my journey of doing 100 squats a day, I was completely unaware of proper form. However, it's essential to be cautious, as even home workouts can be risky, especially if rushed. Therefore, it's crucial to prioritize learning about proper form. If you have a personal trainer, they'll emphasize form extensively. Similarly, instructors in gym fitness classes will always stress the importance of form, not to annoy you, but to ensure your safety and the effectiveness of your workout. Safety should always be the top priority.

So, consider adding squats to your daily workout routine if you think they could make a difference. They could be the key to overcoming a fitness plateau or tackling stubborn fat that's been resistant to other methods.

Your body can become accustomed to the same exercises, so it's essential to mix things up to keep challenging yourself and see results. Exercises like squats, which test your body weight resistance, are excellent additions to any routine. Personally, I swear by squats, and if you haven't tried them yet, you might just find that you'll love them too.

In this book, I have touched on being mentally fit. We know exercise can compliment this, but being a seeker of wisdom can as well. There is a quote that I'm going to focus on that comes from a philosopher by the name of René Descartes. For some of you who are philosophy students, you may be very familiar with Descartes, Mr. "I think, therefore I am."

However, I'm going to focus on a different quote of his, one for which he is at least credited, although its origin isn't clear. It reminds me of an encounter I had related to fitness. According to Descartes, "Whenever anyone has offended me, I try to raise my soul so high that the offense can't reach it."

One day, a young lady reached out to me inquiring about personal training. I noticed that she lived close to where I conduct fitness classes. So, I extended an invitation for her to join one of my classes as my complimentary guest. This way, she could experience one of my workouts before making the investment.

She explained to me that she tends to avoid gyms due to some negative experiences related to her weight. She's had people say mean things to her while she was trying to work out, which made her self-conscious. Her story reminded me of that quote from Descartes. Sometimes, we allow ourselves to be so offended that it leaves us in a place of shame and isolation. When we do that, we give away our power so much that we fail to celebrate our efforts.

She was so worried about what people would think, what people would say, that she was not taking time to celebrate the fact that she was taking steps forward. At least she was trying to. Interestingly, even with meeting with me one-on-one, I sensed that she was trying to talk her way out of it. She was dedicated to this story of being self-conscious, feeling like she's too big, feeling like she's let herself go.

Yes, we can worry about how we gain weight all day long. We can even worry about how we've let ourselves go. We can also worry about the people who will laugh and pick at us. We can make that the focus, or we can focus on the fact that I'm doing something today because I can't go back and change what led to my experience in this moment. However, I can make the best of right now. I can silence any naysayers, and I can advance forward. My focus is on living healthier, not someone else's opinion of how I have handled my life up to this point.

That's what you must hold on to. You can't dwell on the offense because people will attempt to offend you, even when you rock and crush your goals. *People will always have something to say*. My mom and I used to talk about our weight loss journey. We realized that when people saw us after losing weight, they could wonder about our well-being: Are they doing okay financially? Are they managing to eat well?

The moral of the story is this: When you're bigger, they're going to talk about you. Even when you've lost the weight and you look and feel fabulous, they'll still wonder if something negative is going on with you.

Bottom line, people will always have an angle. If you invest your energy in being offended by all those outside voices, then your soul will be easily wounded.

So, carry it high, as Descartes taught us. So high, that your focus remains steadfast, whether people are your cheerleaders or your critics. Keep your soul so high that it lifts you towards your health and your healing. Keep it THAT high! So high, that no one can touch it, and no person can destroy it—not even you.

Squat Challenge

Option 1:

1 Minute Lateral Squat Hops

Option 2:

2 Sets of 30-second Lateral Squat Hops
Rest In-Between Sets for 30-seconds

Wise Act

Take a moment to check in with your soul. If the term *soul* feels awkward, simply check in within. Ask yourself some key questions: Are you mindful of your health? Is your work environment toxic? Are you harboring toxicity within yourself or projecting it onto others? Are you staying hydrated? Are you experiencing tension in your body due to poor posture or unhealthy habits? Are your breaths shallow? The purpose is to be honest with yourself, identifying areas needing balance and making it a priority to address them. Consider making this self-reflection a monthly, if not daily, routine.

49

"It's easier to notice things we dislike about others, but it requires maturity to recognize our own shortcomings just as easily."

Chapter 7
Sometimes, It's Us

I had a job one year where I traveled the United States. I was talking to my mom one day and reflecting on some of my memories from the experience. I am one of those people who really hates loud noises from neighbors. I've always appreciated peace and quiet in my personal living space even as a kid, but as an adult, I was more extreme about it. I was telling my mom how I would complain about noise in my hotels. Interestingly, during my travels, I was cooking breakfast early one morning and I caused the smoke detector to go off.

It did not just go off in my room. It went off throughout the hotel. I mean a loud siren that lasted a good 2-3 minutes. I felt so bad. I was beyond embarrassed. It was barely 5 AM. Yet, there I was, the one who is usually quick to complain about noise, being the noise-maker. My mom said that goes to show that "sometimes, it's us." Those words stuck with me.

I apologized profusely to the front desk and they laughed and said it doesn't happen all the time, but it definitely happens. And just as I did not intend to be noisy that day, some of the people I may have complained about may not have intended to be noise-makers either.

One thing we are all good at is communicating about when someone or something has angered or annoyed us, but we often fail to accept the fact that there are people out there that we have upset. People who we have made a toxic and negative impact on. And a lot like my early morning breakfast, the offense could have been unintentional or intentional. Either way, it is important for us to know that sometimes, it really is us.

Just as we have impressions of others, we too are giving off impressions. Not that we should live to please people or censor our authentic selves, but I think it is wise to purpose to reflect on the question: How are others experiencing me? *It's easier to notice things we dislike about others, but it requires maturity to recognize our own shortcomings just as easily.* It takes even more maturity to openly put words to the offenses that we have unleashed onto others with the intent of making those wrongs right.

Years ago, I attempted to right my own wrongs. I taught for 15 years before realizing I wanted to take a break from teaching in 2020. While I am confident I left many of my students with good memories, I know for a fact that I missed the mark with some students as well. I was at a point of severe burnout in 2019. When I knew that my interactions with students were not consistently healthy, I knew that the wise thing for me to do was to step away for a while.

After a three-year hiatus, I got back into teaching. The time away helped me to realize where my ego got in the way of me being a helpful and encouraging guide for my students. This comes naturally for me when speaking or leading fitness sessions. It even came naturally with my college students who I felt were sincerely trying. I noticed my ego emerging when I caught students cheating.

Instead of recognizing that many students cheat due to their own fears, I adopted a "no one is going to get over on me" attitude. As a result, I created a lot of unnecessary stress for myself and I robbed those students of the opportunity to see themselves in a more empowered light. Stepping away helped me to see that sometimes it wasn't the student, but me who fell short of turning an instance of cheating into a profound shift in mindset for myself as well as the student.

I had to remind myself of my own words and advice during my hiatus. I often tell students that they come to college to learn, not to show off how much they know. I know a focus on earning good grades is the end goal, but the journey is the true experience of learning in my book. As an educator, if I too place a hyper-focus on grades, I rob my students of leaning into the beautiful journey of learning.

The journey of realizing that you don't have to hide your fear of writing behind the words of someone else or, these days, Artificial Intelligence. Like the philosophers we study, I remind students that their mind is worthy of being amplified. Philosophy is filled with unique thinkers, once considered insane. Yet today, colleges all over the world study these so-called lunatic minds.

I am so thankful that I took that much-needed break, for it pointed my heart back to where it was my first year as a college teacher. Where my focus was to help and inspire the students entrusted to me. Additionally, the time away illuminated my mind to the fact that my burnout in 2019 was self-imposed.

The students weren't the problem. It was me. But I'm back to teaching and my mind is renewed. Sure, some students are still cheating, but my response to it has changed. It has evolved to a healthier place that enables me to enjoy my work by focusing on the purpose of me being there, which is to help students realize their potential, and not to nurture my ego as the cheat police.

The next time you're feeling burnout with a situation, ask yourself: Is it the situation? Or, is it me? Because sometimes, it is you, and if that is the case, you can transform the situation by shifting how you see and experience it.

Squat Challenge

Option 1:

50 Bodyweight Squats

Option 2:

5 Sets of 10 Bodyweight Squats
Rest In-Between Sets for 15-seconds

Wise Act

Focus on the message of Michael Jackson's *Man in the Mirror*. Look up the lyrics, find a line that resonates, then watch a live performance of Jackson singing it on YouTube. As you watch, reflect on why that line resonated and take one actionable step to apply its message. Share your experience with me on the *Squat Wisely* Facebook page.

57

"Whether people are there or not, you still have yourself."

Chapter 8
Made-Up Mind

This message will not be for everyone. I'm going to use the F word, meaning fat, not to be offensive but to cater to a very specific audience of people who need to be reminded of the power that they have within themselves to change their situation. Furthermore, I want to address this topic because I want to encourage people to eliminate the excuses in their lives that they use to justify why they can't take steps forward when it comes to their self-care and their health. Oftentimes, you'll hear people say, "I know I need to lose weight." Or, "I know I've gained weight, but I can't afford to eat healthy. I can't afford a gym membership. I can't afford a personal trainer." They are very focused on the excuses, but I want to destroy most of those common excuses today.

Yes, I am a fitness professional; I am a personal trainer. But the reality is you don't need a personal trainer to lose weight; you don't need a gym membership to lose weight; you don't need to spend over $100 a week on healthy groceries to lose weight. The only thing you need to conquer your fitness goals is a willing and made-up mind.

Actually, I had a personal trainer that quit on me. So, when my personal trainer quit on me, did that mean that I need to now quit on myself? Was my goal based on having a cheerleader or was it based on motivation that was deep within me to see that goal through?

Many of us, every single day, whether we're indulging in all the doughnuts we can find, drinking all the soda we can find, or consuming all the fried foods we can find - with each plate, many of you mentally say, "I don't need this." I've been around people who have said, "I don't need to be eating this." Yet, they still proceed to eat it.

When people ask me questions as a personal trainer, they want my opinion about diet. Truth be told, if you are only certified as a personal trainer and you're not a nutritionist or registered dietitian, you're not supposed to give meal plans. However, we can provide advice. The main advice that I give people is to embrace common sense. Remember, you are more powerful than you realize. The steps that you took to gain the weight, you need that same level of consistency to lose it.

You know that you're fat, so now what are you going to do? Are you going to continue to fill your plate with food that you know you should not be ingesting, or are you going to be mindful, and are you going to ask yourself, "Does this plate lead to the person that I want to be, or does it further fuel the person that I don't want to be?" Everything begins and ends with you.

Yes, a lot of people out here will hire a personal trainer, but so many people who pay that money to hire a personal trainer, as soon as the session has ended, they basically throw their money away by the habits they keep beyond the personal training session. You can't pay your way to consistent results, regardless of what your income is. Regardless of how much money you're willing to kick out on a gym membership. If you are not personally committed and consistent, you'll never see the results.

Now that you acknowledge your current situation, you also recognize that you have the power to change it. Every time you eat, ask yourself, "Does this lead to the results I want, or does it further fuel the results I don't want?" Can I take a walk in my neighborhood? Can I find a workout video on YouTube and do it at home? When you have a made-up mind, you're not concerned about the cost of a gym membership or a personal trainer because you already know there are plenty of free resources available to help you achieve your goals.

So, I want you to embrace that. Make things happen in your life, and be your own cheerleader. That way, *whether people are there or not, you still have yourself,* and the results you desire WILL soon follow.

Squat Challenge

Option 1:

1 Minute Sumo Squat Heel Lifts

Option 2:

2 Sets of 30-second Sumo Squat Heel Lifts
Rest In-Between Sets for 30-seconds

Wise Act

Set a **specific** goal by marking a day on your calendar for *No Excuses Day* within the next 7 days. On this day, make up your mind to commit to a specific task related to fitness, launching your business, or any personal goal. Remember, progress begins with just one step. Embracing excuses holds you back, but progress begins the moment you take action.

63

"Some days, we are well-rested; yet tired."

Chapter 9
When You Get Tired

We all know that working out can make you tired at times. As we live longer, we come to understand that tiredness isn't limited to physical exhaustion alone. Nor is it limited to a lack of rest. *Some days, we are well-rested; yet tired.* Some days, the true weight isn't measured by the person standing on the scale, but rather by the invisible burden of simply existing and navigating life's challenges.

Over the years, I have known friends who could no longer bear the unshakable weight of being tired. So, they tragically took their own lives, seeking relief from their suffering.

Maybe you have been there. Maybe you have had days where you've had to pull over on the side of the road. Your car was not broken down, but inside you were.

So, you pulled over, simply to cry and ask God why. Maybe you have faced days where you counted all of your blessings and you realized you should only have room to be thankful and filled with joy, yet you struggled to feel that way within. You may even have people in your life that you love and love you back. You could enjoy a dream career that people are envious of, but even that is not enough to shake off the bouts of tiredness that come.

I have been tired in the gym. I have been tired due to a lack of sleep. But I too have felt the weight of tiredness that comes from simply living this life. This is not a chapter to tell you how to shake it off. It is my belief that as long as we are human beings, we will all face days where we're just tired. I see it as a natural part of our human experience.

If anything, this chapter is here to remind you that you are not alone. While we seldom discuss our tiredness openly, I believe in acknowledging my limitations when it's appropriate. For instance, my personal training clients often express admiration for my exercise performance. However, I always make it clear that I have my own limitations. There are exercises I avoid or modify for safety reasons, as excelling in many exercises doesn't make me immune to limitations.

So, just like I remind my clients that I am just like them, filled with limitations too, know that when you get tired, I might be tired too. Even your family or close friends, they could be tired as well.

Over the years, one of my friends, who later committed suicide, would call me after we graduated high school. This was when I was focused on my new college life, and since I did not live in the same city, I lost touch. However, when I found out he died, my mind went to all the times he was trying to reach out to me, but I was too busy or too distracted to connect.

He could have been looking for a distraction from his tired mind, but I wasn't available. I am not suggesting that I could have changed his mind, but I do know that I could have purposed to at least engage and spend more time. The next time you're feeling tired, allow that to be a reminder that you are not the only one. Maybe someone's unusual silence is their way of letting you know. Or, maybe them calling and you being too busy is your cue to check-in.

When I was younger, I was glued to my phone, constantly chatting with friends. However, as I transitioned into adulthood, my desire for constant connection diminished, and I embraced my introverted nature more fully. While it's true that I've become more introverted over time, the loss of friends to suicide has profoundly impacted my perspective. It has taught me the importance of reaching out when someone is on my mind or appears to be reaching out themselves. Even as an introvert, I can always engage with others authentically and genuinely, in a way that feels sincere for me.

For example, I enjoy old-school snail mail. While technology has somewhat pushed us away from it, receiving a letter in the mail remains a beautiful gesture, especially these days because it's so rare. I know it can be hard for us to see beyond our own tired days, but perhaps our burden can be lightened by recognizing ourselves in others and showing up in our own way when we can.

Squat Challenge

Find a Squat Workout on YouTube that looks interesting and follow along.

Wise Act

The next time you experience tiredness that sleep cannot fix, go on YouTube and look up the *Golden Girls* Theme Song. As you listen to that song, whoever comes to mind, mail that person a handwritten letter or card. If they're no longer with us, do something to honor their life and memory.

69

"Pain has no respect for when it hits you."

Chapter 10
Silent Battles

I hope that when you are reading this message, you are well and in great health within your body and mind. If not, maybe this chapter will ignite feelings of gratitude and joy, because I want to focus on kindness. I want to include a quote often attributed to Plato: "Be kind, for everyone you meet is fighting a battle." Despite debate over the origin of this quote, for me, the message is more important than the messenger. I like this quote because of the distinction that it makes about *everyone* that you meet. In my mind, that has a lot to do with when you're out in public and you come in contact with random strangers.

You never know what people are dealing with as you travel alongside them on highways or stand beside them in stores. Some may be experiencing wonderful joys, while others may be contemplating suicide. Again, we just don't know.

In my interactions with college students, I often introduce an act of kindness assignment. This task prompts reflection on the quote regarding the silent battles that some may face. I've had students give away free hugs, and they've embraced being a Walking Fortune Cookie by distributing encouraging messages to unsuspecting strangers.

Like my students, take a moment to contemplate the concept of kindness and how you can seize more opportunities to express it. Consider the possibility that the person who smiled at you in line or assisted you at Starbucks may be grappling with profound challenges. They could be silently battling feelings of hopelessness, coping with a traumatic loss, or struggling to put food on the table.

The intent is not to assume or ask strangers about their struggles. Instead, it is to simply be reminded that just as things could be heavy on your mind, the same could be true for those you encounter in public. If we keep this in mind, it will help us to rethink how we interact with others. This shifts our focus away from ourselves and opens our eyes to opportunities to extend compassion to those who we would normally overlook.

I have a story that I'll never forget. I was out one day, heading to an appointment. I like to give myself a lot of time because I don't like being right on time for meetings. So, this was one of those days where I was early, so I went to get a snack from the gas station.

I was proud of myself on this day because sometimes, you can be annoyed when you're in the store and people seem to be wasting time. Or, if you get the sense that the attendant is not being attentive to you, then you can get frustrated. It was one of those situations, but I was not annoyed. I was in a positive frame of mind, and I feel like my mind was in the right place--the place that it needed to be for what I was about to witness.

I was next in line to check out, and the lady working the register steps out from behind the counter. She starts to hug the person who was in front of me, and she's just hugging her, and it is clear that she's being very consoling and nurturing toward her. This went on for a few minutes. Naturally, I wanted to check out with the items that I had, but I was very patient and calm. Of course, I didn't know the full details. All I know is that the woman who was working there, she stopped what she was doing. She wasn't even concerned about what was going on at the gas station at that time. And she focused all of her energy, all of her attention onto this woman. When the woman she was consoling walked away, the gas station attendant said to me, "You know, her father just died."

As I witnessed the attendant stop her focus on business to hug someone who desperately needed a hug in that moment, it touched me deeply and took my mind to a place where I better appreciated how fortunate I am to still have my mom and my dad with me.

A day could come where you could be that person in the gas station. You could be that someone who is in desperate need of a random shoulder to cry on. *Pain has no respect for when it hits you.* You could be in the gas station with people, who are annoyed and they just want to buy their gas, get their cigarettes, and go!

I'm so glad I didn't have that hurried mindset in that moment. I'm glad that I was just silent and patient because one day somebody may have to do that same thing for me. It's great when we can turn to what's familiar; it's great when we can call our relatives and our close friends, but pain comes unexpectedly. It can strike at the most awkward, the most inappropriate time, and you would be thankful if you had enough people around you to understand that, like this kind gas station attendant did.

Again, "Be kind, for everyone you meet is fighting a battle." For those of you reading this, you could be facing your own battles right at this moment, and reading this quick message may be an escape for you. Perhaps listening to music or working out serves as an escape from the battles you're fighting.

I'm sure some of you have heard this before: they say the best way to heal your depression is to try to help heal someone else's. We can achieve this through a kind gesture, shifting our focus away from ourselves and onto others.

Many years ago, while I was an undergraduate student at Georgia State University (GSU), majoring in broadcast journalism, we had a group project. Our task was to develop our own news story. We decided to focus on a park close to GSU, interestingly named Hurt Park.

For our story, we chose to highlight the presence of hurting and homeless individuals in Hurt Park. Despite legal restrictions against their residency, many found themselves living there due to limited options. Our project aimed to explore their experiences, focusing on the stories of individuals like one man who left a lasting impression on me.

Despite being college students aiming for a good grade, our decision to stop and talk to him gave him a voice to express his pain. It allowed him to share his experience as a homeless person living with AIDS in Hurt Park.

Sometimes, the random act of kindness is kindness itself. It doesn't require spending money. Simply listening or amplifying someone's voice by sharing their pain--that is the kindness. We shouldn't always measure everything by its monetary value. Our currency lies in our caring and our concern, and it speaks volumes when we extend that to a complete stranger.

As you go about your travels each day, try to remember to bring kindness with you. Try to remember to notice those who often go unnoticed, acknowledge people's pain. Even when it's not someone who you would call a friend or relative. The inconvenience of pain can lead us to lean on the unfamiliar. The stranger you would typically ignore is now your main source of support. Yes, the stranger becomes not only a friend but the strength and understanding that will carry you through.

Back in the day, I used to read the *Chicken Soup for the Soul* series. It's a collection of short stories with profound meanings to inspire you. One of the stories that I read ended with a line that I now use when I give people cards. Under my signed name I include the words, "Who you are makes a difference." For you reading this, who you are makes a difference. While I don't have a card or Hallmark in the mail just for you, allow this chapter to be my Hallmark to you.

The next time you're in a rush and find yourself frustrated by delays or people seeming to waste time, pause for a moment. Reflect on the possibility that those around you might be facing their own silent battles. Your kindness in that moment could be the difference maker. Carry that awareness with you as you navigate through your day. It may offer you the same compassion from strangers when life throws its challenges your way.

Squat Challenge

Option 1:

1 Minute Alternating Squat Kicks

Option 2:

2 Sets of 30-second Alternating Squat Kicks
Rest In-Between Sets for 15-seconds

Wise Act

Give authentically by Paying it Forward to a *stranger*. It's one of the best ways to train yourself on how to give without a catch. You won't expect a call, a thank-you card, or for that person to return a favor. I still remember the few times when strangers made me a recipient of their kindness--it brightened a dull day for me. So, be that light for someone else. Who YOU ARE makes a profound difference. Always remember that.

"I have fulfilled my assignment."

Conclusion: It's always something...GREAT!

Wow! You guys have no idea the tears I have shed. I was afforded many opportunities to embrace my own advice as I got closer to finishing this book. I had to *Write it OUT*. I had to accept moments where I was the problem. I had to reflect on times when I was not mindful of the *Silent Battles* of others. I faced days when I was tired, but sleep could not resolve it. So many distractions came my way just before completing this work. I vowed to write a short book with an impact, reminding myself that less is more.

The impact struck me before it could reach you. Life's lessons emphasized the power of leading by example through both my words and actions. I was reminded of the importance of transparency in my writing and the need to acknowledge moments where I resisted my inner wisdom.

I can always tell when I'm on the right track in life. The moments where I'm most focused and productive are also the times when I am challenged the most. For example, almost without fail, when I purpose to get up extra early to get ahead on work, my computer forces a restart. The Wi-Fi starts coming in and out. Many of us have faced those small annoyances that attempt to make you feel defeated for trying.

When those times happen, I learned to change my language. I would often say out of frustration, "It's always something!" Don't get me wrong, I still say that to myself when I'm annoyed, but I catch myself and say, "It's always something…GREAT" instead. I'm still irritated by the situation, but I'm training my mind to deal with it from a higher place.

Just as I faced challenges while completing this book, I've come to realize that even when life attempts to break us down, there's always something great happening within us. It gives us an opportunity to be flexible yet focused on executing our plans, regardless of the obstacles presented. While my book may only reach the eyes of one person, if it helps that one person, the obstacles I faced were worth it; for *I have fulfilled my assignment.*

Some days I had to push my feelings aside to train my clients. Surprisingly, those were the days they raved about the workouts the most. In each session, I typically incorporate some form of squats. I used to fear that they would find it repetitive. Just because I love squats doesn't mean they will be a favorite for everyone. Honestly, most individuals I train have a love-hate relationship with squats. They dislike the burn but love it for its benefits at the same time.

Wisdom is kind of like that. We love the wisdom we gain, but some of the life-lessons that wisdom is birthed from burns worse than any squat ever could. Just as we understand the benefits of the burn from the exercises we perform, we grow in maturity when we understand our life experiences in the same way.

The pain is not for nothing. It's to make you stronger in body and mind. It's to help you to see the parallels between our fitness life and our human experience. You are strong, even when you are weak. In fitness, we talk about working to a point of failure. It sounds like a defeat, but it's actually a strength tactic. You are learning and building yourself up even when you fail. You gain strength by embracing your weaknesses. The next time you work out, keep this in mind and you will *Squat Wisely* every time.

Thank you again, for investing your time in my work. I hope that in some small way you have gained some wisdom while reading this book. If you'd like to connect, don't hesitate to reach out to me through the *Squat Wisely* Facebook page.

*"**Wisdom** is the principal thing; therefore get wisdom: and with all thy getting get understanding."*

Proverbs 4:7